Finding-Out Books

WETLANDS
Bogs, Marshes, and Swamps

By Lewis Buck

Illustrated by Grambs Miller

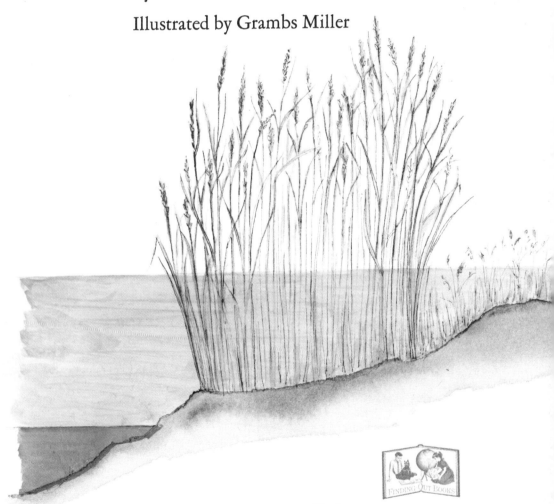

Parents' Magazine Press · New York

Library of Congress Cataloging in Publication Data

Buck, Lewis A.
   Wetlands: bogs, marshes, and swamps.

   (A Finding-out book)
   SUMMARY: Traces the development and describes the
characteristics of bogs, marshes, and swamps.
   1. Wetland ecology–Juvenile literature. 2. Wetlands–Juvenile literature.   [1. Wetland ecology.
2. Ecology]   I. Miller, Grambs, illus. II. Title.
QH541.5.M3B83   574.5'2632   73-5711
ISBN 0-8193-0702-5

Contents

1. What's-its-name

When most of us look around the places where we live we see mainly dry land. Another word for dry land is earth. We call our home planet Earth.

Look at a globe of the Earth. Compare the size of all the dry land areas on the globe to all the areas covered by water—the oceans, seas, and lakes. Which areas are greater?

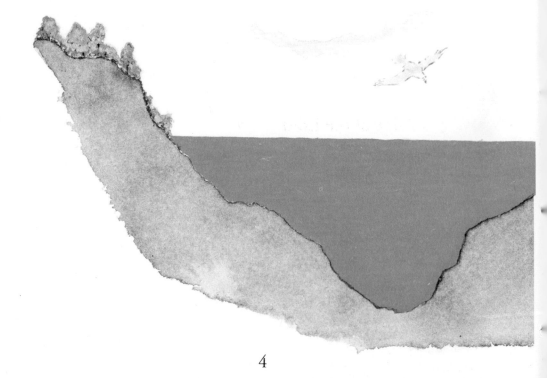

Perhaps we should call our home planet Water.

If the Earth had no mountains and valleys under the oceans and on the land, we would all have to be very good swimmers. The sea would be about a mile and a half deep everywhere.

Water does cover the land in some places. These places are not deep enough to be called by watery names like pond, lake, sea, or ocean. But they are deep enough so that they are not called fields and forests. We call these places marshes, swamps, and bogs. The name we give them all together is *wetlands*.

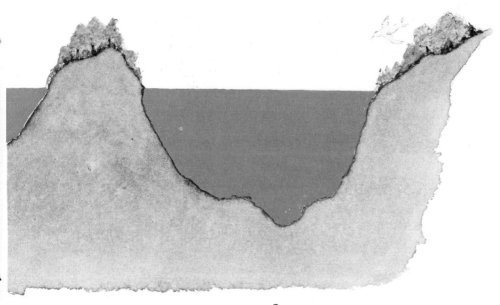

Places where water stands upon the land and grasses grow are marshes. Not all the plants that live in marshes are grasses, but to most people they look like grasses, at least from a distance.

Wetlands where trees are growing with their roots beneath the water are called swamps.

Marsh

Swamp

Sometimes men, or beavers, may dam a woodland
stream, and the water will flood the surrounding
forest. For a while such places may look like a
swamp. But the trees will not live another year.
Only certain trees, like the mangrove and the
cypress, can live with their roots always under water
and make a swamp.

Perhaps the strangest wetland of all is the quaking bog. From its edge you can see that the bog is covered with low bushes. The ground looks solid and a little lumpy. But when you walk on the ground you find that it bounces, and bushes some distance away will shake. And your feet will get wet.

If you are not careful, the rest of you will get wet, too. The real floor of the bog may be fifteen feet below you. You are standing on a layer of plants that are floating on water.

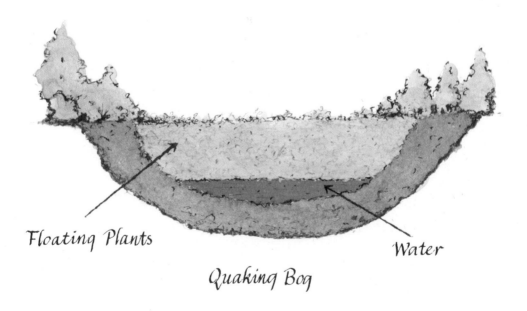

Floating Plants

Water

Quaking Bog

2. The Between-lands

Indians called marshes "between-land." This meant "something that is neither land nor water."

The largest marsh in the United States, the Florida Everglades, was named the River of Grass by the Seminole Indians. That sounds as if the marsh were both land and water.

All wetlands are places that are slowly changing from water to dry land. It may take hundreds or even thousands of years, but every pond or lake is changing to a forest.

In places like our western prairies, where there is not enough rainfall each year for trees to grow, the changing stops when the land is covered with grass.

Let's see how these changes come about. We'll

use a pond for an example. The same things happen to lakes, but the larger the body of water, the longer it takes for the changes to happen.

First of all, for a pond you have to have a hole in the ground. When it rains, water runs into the hole.

But is that all that runs in? How about dirt? Little grains of dirt are pushed into the hole by the rain water. If the rain is heavy enough, large pieces of dirt are pushed in. After many years the rain would wash in enough dirt to fill the hole.

Eel Grass   Waterweed   Broad-leaf Pondweed

Something else is happening at the same time. Things other than dirt are getting into the hole and making it fill up faster. Plants and animals are moving in.

The first plants may live completely under water. They may be so small that you need a microscope to see them. Or they may have roots in the dirt at the bottom of the pond and long stems and leaves. But they do not need to stick their leaves out into the air.

We call these *submergent* plants. They seem to

Bladderwort   Ruffle-leaf Pondweed

belong more to the pond than to the marsh. But they do grow and make new plants and die, and the dead ones sink to the bottom of the pond and help build up the soil.

Then come plants that are rooted to the bottom, with their stems, leaves, and flowers standing up above the water. They could not live if the water did not cover their roots at least part of the time, but their tops need the air. We call these *emergent* plants. They are the beginning of the marsh.

Emergent Plants

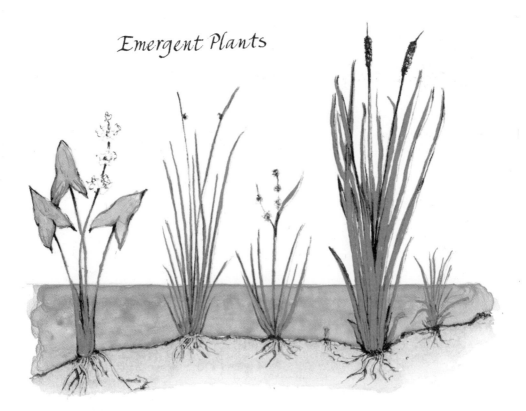

As more and more plants die and become part of the soil, there is less and less room for water. The soil becomes firmer. Bushes and trees can grow, and we have a swamp.

As time goes on and more dead plants are added to the soil and more dirt washes in, the ground will become higher and drier. Trees that do not need wet soil all the time will take the places of the swamp trees. Then we will have a forest.

Different kinds of animals find homes among different kinds of plants. As land plants take the place of water plants, land animals take the place of water animals.

In order to live, both plants and animals need food, shelter, and room to grow. The plants and animals that live together in one place and provide food for each other make up a *community*.

Some wetland communities are open to the sky and the wind and seem to invite visitors to drop in. Among the many visitors that do drop in to these marshes are flocks of ducks and geese and blackbirds.

Other wetland communities, like bogs and cypress swamps, are quiet, secret places where most people do not feel at home.

3. Wetlands from the Past

If you live in New England, or around the Great Lakes, or in southern Canada, you should be able to find someone who can lead you to a bog. Your guide may call the bog a *muskeg,* the old Indian name for this kind of soft ground.

Do not go alone. The way a bog grows makes it dangerous for a person who has not learned its secrets.

Muskegs are found in places that were covered by ice many, many years ago. About 10,000 years ago the ice began to melt. It left behind in the ground many large, steep-sided holes filled with icy water. In these lakes and ponds the muskegs started.

The ground was almost all rock. The loose dirt had been scraped away by the ice. Rain added water to the holes, but much of it went back into the air as mist and vapor. No streams flowed into or out of the lakes. The water did not move.

Because the water was so still, even tiny things that fell into the lakes did not wash away. Slowly they sank to the bottom.

Ice Block melting

By digging carefully into the muck of a bog and studying the different layers of plant matter that have settled there over hundreds of years, scientists have been able to find out that different kinds of forests grew there in the past. These different kinds

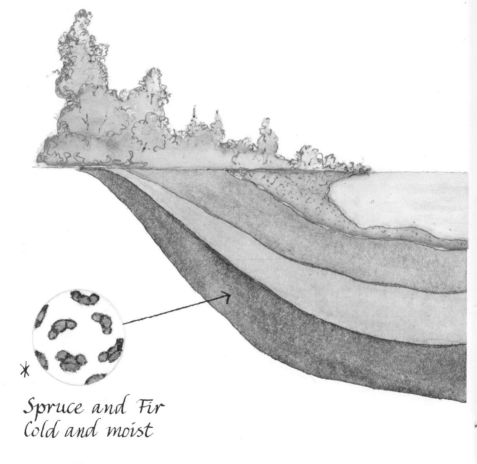

*Spruce and Fir
Cold and moist*

✳ *Pollen grains enlarged*

of forests showed what the climate had been like. Layers from spruce and fir trees meant that the climate had been cold and wet. Layers from oak and hickory trees meant that the climate was warm and dry when they were growing.

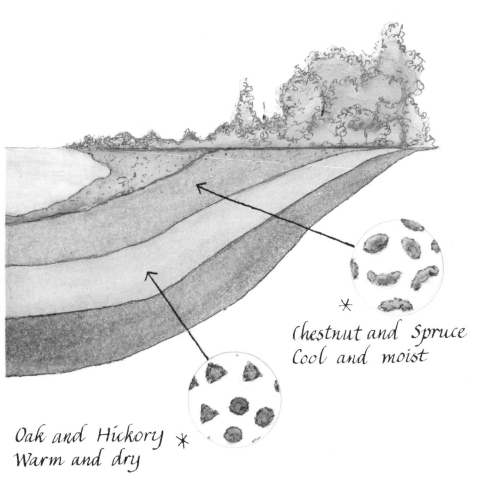

* Chestnut and Spruce
Cool and moist

Oak and Hickory *
Warm and dry

One of the first emergent plants in a young lake is the water lily. In still water the long stem lifts flowers and leaves to float on the surface of the water.

The plant that really starts to build a bog is one that looks much like a grass. It is called a sedge.

One way to tell a sedge from a grass is to look closely at the stem. Grass stems are round and hollow and have swollen joints. Most sedge stems have three sides and are solid in the middle and the joints are not swollen.

At the water's edge the roots of the sedges grow so they become tangled together in a mat.

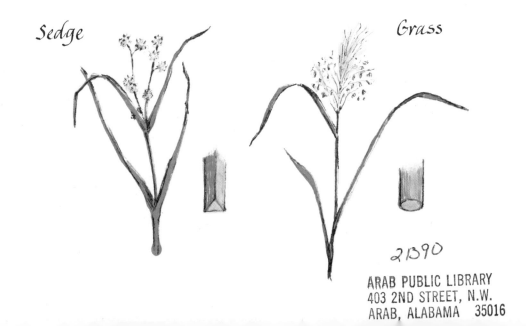

Sedge   *Grass*

Sphagnum Moss

The next bog builder is the plant called peat moss, or sphagnum. It is a soft, feathery plant that loves water. It sucks up about sixteen times its own weight in water. In the summer all this water in the moss keeps the bog cool. The coolness of the bog slows down the growth of the plants that live there.

Peat moss grows among the roots of the sedges and makes the floating mat thicker. Larger plants take root in the mat and make it even stronger: low

bushes with names like leatherleaf, lambkill, Labrador tea, and bog rosemary. They look much alike, perhaps because they all belong to the same plant family, the heaths.

The mat of roots, stems, and peat moss spreads farther onto the lake. The mat keeps the sunlight from shining down into the water. Since all plants need sunlight in order to grow, submergent plants cannot grow under the mat.

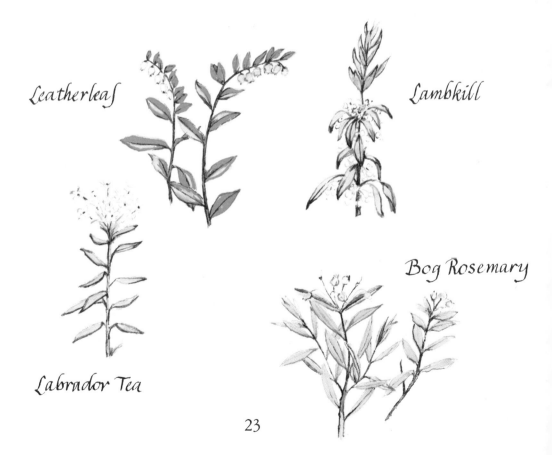

Leatherleaf

Lambkill

Bog Rosemary

Labrador Tea

23

As new things are growing on top of the mat, old pieces of plant are dying and dropping from the underside and sinking to the bottom of the lake. More and more dead plants fall to the bottom.

Part of the strangeness of the bog is that these dead plants do not decay all the way. The coldness of the water slows down the growth even of the smallest plants, called *bacteria,* that cause plants and animals to decay. In order to do their work of decaying, bacteria also need oxygen. But the bog water is so still that almost no oxygen gets to the bottom.

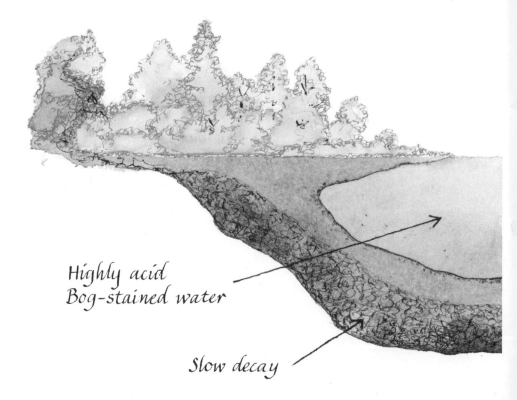

Highly acid
Bog-stained water

Slow decay

The dead plants pile up. They become packed tightly together. They become the stuff we call peat. The water turns dark brown and very sour, or acid.

Some bogs are so old that they have filled to the top with peat. There is no longer any open water, and the bog no longer quakes.

In some countries the peat is cut and dried in blocks to be burned in stoves. In the United States, loose peat moss is packed in large bags and sold to people who have gardens. See if you can find out what a gardener does with peat moss.

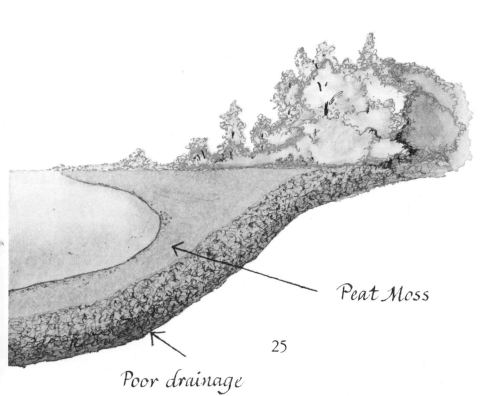

Peat Moss

Poor drainage

4. Who's At Home?

A bog is not an easy place to live in. Only a few kinds of plants are able to grow in the cold, acid water. Animals that eat plants do not have a lot to choose from there. So not many different kinds of animals are found in the bog.

Large animals, like bear, moose, and deer may wander into a bog looking for food. But they do not stay long—unless they make a mistake. Then they may stay forever.

26

A long time ago some very large animals made the mistake of coming too close to the middle of a bog. They fell through the moss and sedges. Scientists have dug from bogs the bones of animals unlike any that live in North America today.

Mastodons and woolly mammoths that looked like hairy elephants fell into the bog. So did giant ground sloths and woodland musk oxen. You may find their skeletons in natural history museums today.

You might sometimes see a beaver or a mink or a muskrat in a bog. They can all swim well, and they spend a lot of time in or near the water. But the muskeg is not truly their home.

Mink

Muskrat

Beaver

Snowshoe rabbits, with their big feet, can get around well on the soft, spongy surface, but they too are only visitors.

The only furry animals that seem to be really at home in sphagnum bogs are the water shrew and the bog lemming. Like mice, they tunnel in the moss and are hard to see. You must watch quietly for a long time the way an owl does.

Bullfrogs and pickerel frogs are sometimes found on the sedge mat close to the open water. They breathe air, but they lay their eggs in jelly-like globs

Rabbit

Lemming

Water Shrew

28

in still water. Young frogs are called tadpoles. At first they have tails and live under water. You've probably seen them in an aquarium.

Perhaps most at home are the bog turtles. They are dark, with a bright orange or yellow patch on the head, and only about four inches long when fully grown.

No matter how much you might like the bog turtle, do not take one home with you. There are few of them left. Many of the wet places where they like to live have been drained by people who think wetlands are not useful.

Frog

Bog Turtle

Wiggle-tails

Many birds may pass through the bog on their way north in the Spring and south in the Fall. Only three kinds are likely to nest there—the ring-necked duck, the yellow-bellied flycatcher, and the palm warbler. The duck eats mostly sedge roots and seeds. The other two bog nesters eat insects.

Mosquitoes are one kind of insect that is quite at home in the bog and in other wetlands. Mosquitoes lay their eggs in still water. The young mosquitoes, called wiggle-tails, live under the water until they become adults.

Palm Warbler

Ring-necked Duck

Yellow-bellied Flycatcher

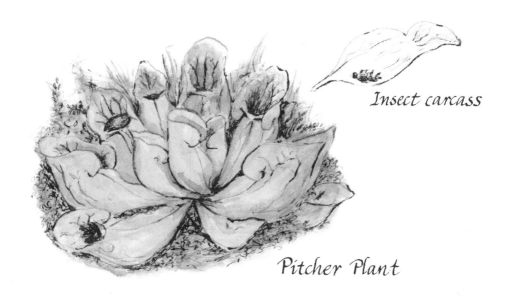

Insect carcass

Pitcher Plant

Birds are not the only things in the bog that eat insects. Some plants add insects to their diets. The plants don't have a mouth and teeth, but they do have a way to suck the juices out of the insects they trap.

The largest of these insect eaters is the pitcher plant. Its name comes from the shape of its leaves, which look a little like water pitchers. Inside the lip of the pitcher grow sharp-pointed, slippery hairs that are aimed down into the pitcher. Insects that crawl into the leaf cannot turn around and crawl out.

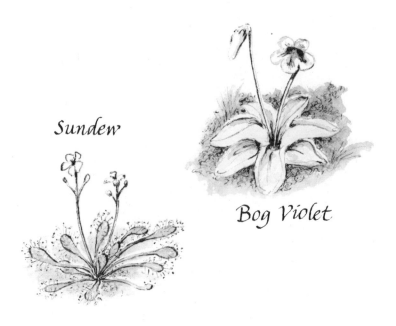

Sundew

Bog Violet

The sundew is such a small plant that most of us do not see it unless it is pointed out to us. When you find one you'll know why it is called sundew. It is sparkling wet-looking, orange and red. Many tiny spikes stick out of its leaves. All the spikes are tipped with a sticky juice. An insect that touches the juice is stuck to the plant for good—or for bad, if you look at things from the insect's point of view.

Also hidden in the moss are some little flowers called bog violets, which are not really violets. Their greasy yellow leaves catch and hold insects for food too.

Pitcher plant and sundew don't sound like fierce names. And who would ever suspect that something called a bog violet would eat insects? You might think that plants called snake-mouth and dragon's-mouth did such things, but they don't. They are orchids that grow quietly in the sphagnum moss. When they bloom in early summer, people who love flowers visit bogs to see their beautiful blossoms.

Dragon's-mouth

Snake-mouth

5. Life in a Duck Factory

In south central Canada and the north central United States are millions of small marshes. Like bogs, they are reminders of times long past.

Large chunks of ice broke off of the sheets of ice that once covered this area. As time went on these chunks of ice were buried under sand and gravel. When the ice finally melted, it left holes in the ground that we now call potholes.

This is part of the *prairies,* or *grasslands,* where there is not enough rainfall each year for forests to grow. In dry years half of the potholes will have no water in them.

Grass once covered the land between the potholes as far as the eye could see. Now farmers raise corn and wheat there. They have drained the

water out of some of the potholes in order to raise more corn and wheat in them.

Still, the potholes that remain are the nesting places of millions of ducks and geese and other waterfowl.

Some potholes are completely covered with emergent plants like arrowhead, burreed, cattails, and bulrushes. Other potholes are large enough to have open water in the middle, with emergent plants around the shore.

Ducks need both kinds of potholes. A pair of ducks may use a small pothole to build their nest in and to raise their young. The tall plants make good hiding places and provide plenty of food.

Ducklings eat the seeds of the bulrush and a smaller plant called smartweed. When they are older they move to the larger potholes where they can eat the leaves, seeds, and roots of the underwater pondweeds. They also like to eat snails and young insects that live in the water.

Not only mosquitoes, but dragonflies, midges, mayflies, damselflies, and some beetles start their lives under water. We do not usually see these young insects (called *larvae*) on our visits to the marsh. They crawl around on the underwater stems of the plants and in the bottom mud. They have no wings, and they do not look at all like their flying parents.

Muskrats may be seen all year round in almost any kind of marsh. These large, brown rats have

hind feet that are partly webbed like a duck's. Their tails are flat on the sides and are used like a rudder to steer them as they swim.

Even if you don't see any muskrats when you visit a marsh, you will probably see one of their lodges. The lodges look like trash heaps. Muskrats cut and pile up many of the same kinds of plants they eat—bulrushes, burreed, and arrowhead. They dig tunnels in this mound of plants for shelter.

6. Downstream

The water in rivers, potholes, and streams is called
fresh water. This does not mean that it is clean
enough for you to drink. In fact, if it flows near our
cities or factories, it is probably polluted by our
sewage. "Fresh" means that the water is not salty
like sea water.

Along slow rivers, where the water spreads out
over low ground, we find other fresh water marshes
and some swamps.

Arrowhead, bulrush, and cattail grow in the river
marshes too. You can see muskrat lodges and hear
the calls of hundreds of blackbirds, just as you did
among the potholes.

In quiet waters where the mud is soft and deep,
we find wide fields of a tall grass called wild rice.
The seeds are eaten by bobolinks and other

Arrowhead

Bulrush

Cattail

Wild Rice

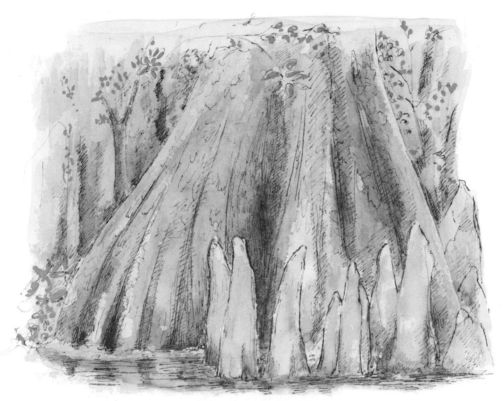

Cyprus "Knees"

blackbirds, by ducks, like the blue-winged teal, and by men.

The swamps do not all look alike. Drier swamps will look much like an ordinary forest. But where water covers the ground all the time you will find trees like the water tupelo, with its swollen trunk, or the bald cypress, with roots growing up in knobs that look like a lot of "knees" poking out of the water.

In the swamps you might catch a glimpse of a wood duck. They build nests in holes in trees high over the water.

Where rivers empty into the ocean, fresh and salt water mix together. We call this mixture *brackish* water.

In brackish water another kind of very tall grass, called reed, builds marshes with its roots. The roots grow in a thick tangle that catches and holds dirt and mud washed down by the river.

Reeds have been used in the past to thatch roofs, to make musical pipes, and even to build small boats. But they may prove to be most useful right where they grow.

Reeds continue to live and grow in some places where other marsh grasses have been killed off by sewage from our cities and factories. Reeds even help to clean up the water when it has been polluted by oil and other wastes.

Reeds

7. The Edge of the Land

To get to many of our seashores you must cross acres of marshland.

Much of the low-lying land along the coast is covered twice each day by the salty water of the sea. When this happens, we say that the tide is high. When the water goes down again, we say the tide is low.

Only a few kinds of emergent plants can stand salty water around their roots for even a short time. So, when we go into one of these salt marshes, we see a great many plants all alike.

But if we look longer, we will see bands, or strips, of different colors through the marsh. Along the channels where the tides come and go, the color is light green. Next comes a wide area of shorter grass that is a little darker green. Then, along the upper edges of the marsh, there grows a strip of still darker green plants.

Where the high tide covers the ground less than half the time, the tall, light-green grass, called cordgrass, is able to grow.

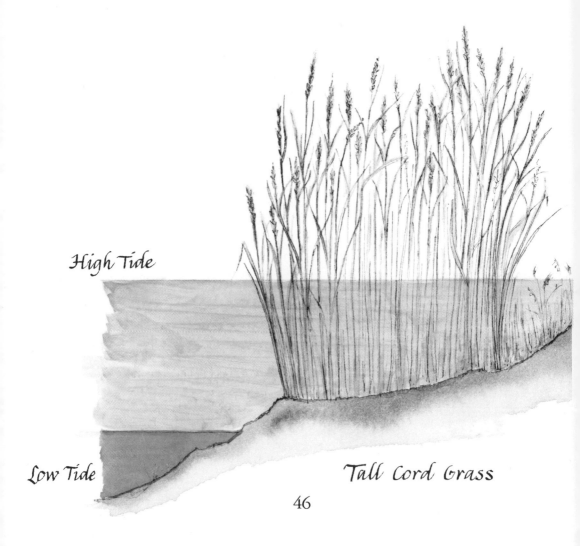

High Tide

Low Tide

Tall Cord Grass

Higher up, where only the highest tides stand for any length of time, the shorter and darker grass, called marsh hay, grows.

The grasses were named by people who used them to make cord for tying things together and to make hay to feed their farm animals.

Marsh Hay

Marsh grasses have strong underground stems and roots. They catch dirt brought down to the sea by rivers as well as sand brought in by ocean waves. They keep the soil from washing away in storms. When the soil gets deeper, other kinds of plants can grow here.

Marshes may burn during dry weather. They may freeze in the winter. But the underground stems live on. They are ready to send up new leaves and put down more roots every spring. They keep the marsh growing from year to year.

The darkest green plants along the drier edges of the salt marsh look like grass from a distance, but they are a kind of rush. Rushes have round stems like grasses, but they are not hollow and they appear to have no joints. Because they turn so dark in the fall these rushes are called *blackrush*.

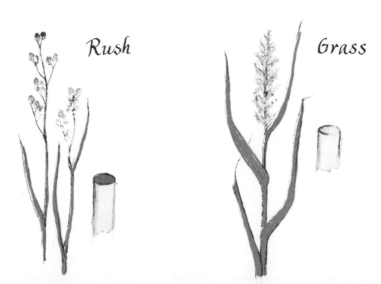

Rush

Grass

Marsh Elder

Just out of reach of the highest tides grow some tall bushes. Called hightide bushes, they mark the edge of the salt marsh and the beginning of dry land.

Marsh grasses need a lot of sunlight. They cannot live in shade. Around the tip of Florida, where the mangrove trees shade out the grasses, we find a salt swamp.

Like the grasses, the mangrove trees have a tangle
of roots. Roots grow down from the trunks and
from the lower branches of the trees. Roots grow
from so many places on the trees that you can
hardly move around in the swamp.

The roots of the mangrove also catch and hold
sand and shells and other things that the tides bring
in. The land builds up. The spreading mangrove
tree starts its own island.

8. What's There to Eat?

Animals that live in salt and brackish marshes stay out of sight most of the time. If you want to find them you have to be patient, like a hunter or a birdwatcher.

You may see a marsh hawk or a short-eared owl flying low over the marsh searching for mice and small birds.

Or you may see herons that visit the marsh to
eat. They are long-legged birds that wade in shallow
water and catch fish and crabs with their long bills.
One heron, the bittern, nests in marshes. When they
stand still, you cannot see them in the tall grass.

You will be lucky if you catch a glimpse of a seaside sparrow or a sharp-tailed sparrow or the clapper rail, all birds that nest and feed in the marsh. They do not fly far even when you scare them up. The sparrows creep about in the grass so that you might mistake them for mice.

Easier to see are black ducks and blue-winged teals that nest and feed in the salt marshes. They are joined in the Fall by many of the waterfowl that nested in the potholes.

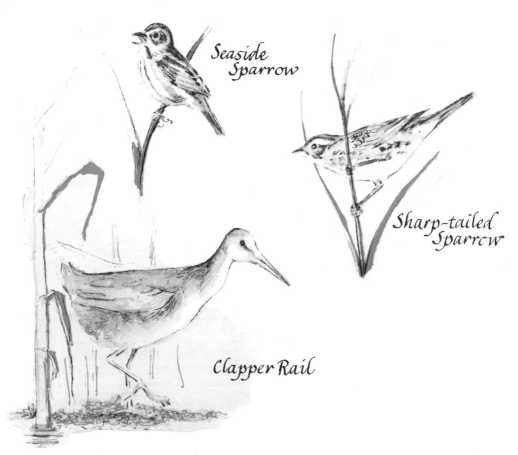

Seaside Sparrow

Sharp-tailed Sparrow

Clapper Rail

You will probably have no trouble finding mosquitoes and tiny biting flies. At least, they will have no trouble finding you. But they are only two out of many kinds of insects that have been found in salt marshes. Most of them will not bother you. Many of them eat plants. Some eat other insects.

Like every other animal in a community, insects are part of a *food chain.* Plants make their own food with the help of sunlight, soil, water, and air. Some animals eat the plants. Other animals eat the animals that eat the plants. Still other animals eat them.

Mosquitoes themselves are an important part of a food chain. Their larvae feed on decaying plants. Small fish, such as the killifish, eat all the larvae they can get. In turn, the killifish are eaten by larger fish from the sea, such as the bluefish. And bluefish are a favorite seafood of many people.

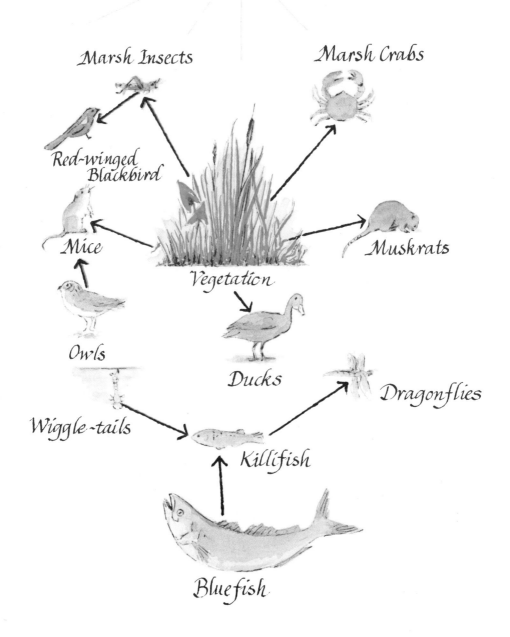

SUN

Marsh Insects

Marsh Crabs

Red-winged
Blackbird

Mice

Muskrats

Owls

Vegetation

Ducks

Wiggle-tails

Killifish

Dragonflies

Bluefish

9. Who Needs It?

Too many people have looked at a marsh and asked, "Who needs it?"

It seems empty and flat and useless. It isn't shady and cool like a forest. It isn't dry like a meadow. You can't have a picnic and play baseball in it. No one really likes to stand around in mud up to his knees and let insects bite him—although duck hunters and birders do it.

So, marshes have been used as dumps. They have been filled with trash, bottles, wrecked cars, and old refrigerators. They have been filled with rocks and dirt to make airports near big cities. They have been covered with cement to make parking lots or to build houses or factories.

And when this is done, the marshes are gone.

But what else goes when the marshes go?
Well, for one thing, the hunter goes. And the

birdwatcher goes. (Each in his own way has loved the marsh and tried to keep it wild.)

More important to most people, when the marshes
go, the seafood fisherman will go because there will
be nothing to catch.

Along the coast, the marsh food chain is part of the food chain of the sea. Young fish of many kinds seek food and shelter in the marshes. Other fish that may not enter the marshes also get food from them.

A salt or a brackish marsh produces more food in a year than a farm the same size would. And you don't have to farm it. In fact, a marsh is better off if you leave it alone.

You just have to let the plants and animals of the marsh live—and die—and decay—and become foodstuff this way.

Each time the tide goes out it carries some of this decaying foodstuff with it to waiting shellfish, like mussels, clams, oysters, shrimp, crabs, and lobsters.

For anyone who can see the fishing boats beyond the marshes, the answer to "Who needs marshes?" is: "People need marshes."

People also need bogs to explore and enjoy. They need potholes to shelter and feed ducks and geese and muskrats. They need swamps and marshes to slow down floods and to keep storm waves from washing away the land.

People need wetlands. But wetlands could get along nicely without people.

Index